The Witch

THE NEW MERMAIDS

General Editor: Brian Gibbons
Professor of English Literature, University of Münster

THE NEW MERMAIDS

The Alchemist
All for Love
Arden of Faversham
The Atheist's Tragedy
Bartholmew Fair
The Beaux' Stratagem
The Broken Heart
Bussy D'Ambois
The Changeling
A Chaste Maid in Cheapside
The Country Wife
The Critic
The Devil's Law-Case
The Double-Dealer
Dr Faustus
The Duchess of Malfi
Eastward Ho!
Edward the Second
Epicoene *or* The Silent Woman
Every Man in His Humour
A Fair Quarrel
An Ideal Husband
The Importance of Being Earnest
The Jew of Malta
The Knight of the Burning Pestle
Lady Windermere's Fan
London Assurance
Love for Love
The Malcontent
The Man of Mode
Marriage A-la-Mode
A New Way to Pay Old Debts
The Plain Dealer
The Playboy of the Western World
The Provoked Wife
The Recruiting Officer
The Relapse
The Revenger's Tragedy
The Rivals
The School for Scandal
She Stoops to Conquer
The Shoemaker's Holiday
The Spanish Tragedy
Tamburlaine
Three Late Medieval Morality Plays
    Mankind
    Everyman
    Mundus et Infans
Thyestes
'Tis Pity She's a Whore
Volpone
The Way of the World
The White Devil
The Witch
A Woman Killed with Kindness
A Woman of No Importance
Women Beware Women